The Under Cover Gardening Guide

How to Grow Your Own
Fresh Organic Vegetables and Fruits
Year-round With Easy to Use
Protective Garden Structures

Nicolette Goff

Table of Contents

INTRODUCTION 1

TEMPORARY PROTECTION WITH CLOCHES.................................4

POLY TUNNELS – PERMANENT CLOCHES 7
WIRE MESH FRAME POLY TUNNEL..8
RAISED BED HOOP FRAME POLY TUNNEL 8

PORTABLE LIGHTWEIGHT CLOCHES 10

ROW COVERS – A MODERN INVENTION 12

COLD FRAMES AND HOT BEDS...13
COLD FRAMES..13
HOT BEDS...17
NATURAL HOT BED 18
OVERWINTERING PLANTS IN A COLD FRAME 19

COLD FRAME GREENHOUSES 21

SUN PIT SOLAR GREENHOUSE..24
CONSTRUCTING A SUN PIT GREENHOUSE......................................25

A SHORT HISTORY OF GREENHOUSES 26

GREENHOUSES TODAY 29
HOW DOES A GREENHOUSE CAPTURE HEAT? 30
BENEFITS OF A GREENHOUSE...30

TYPES OF GREENHOUSES 32

DECIDING ON THE GREENHOUSE 33
TEMPERATURE FACTOR..33
Warm Greenhouse...33
Cool Greenhouse...34
Cold Greenhouse...34
STRUCTURAL DESIGN FACTORS 34
1. Lean-To..35
2. Detached 35
3. Even Span Greenhouse...36
MATERIAL FACTORS 37
1. Glass...37
2. Fiberglass..38

3. Plastic *38*

SITING THE GREENHOUSE **40**

ESSENTIAL TOOLS AND MATERIALS **41**

GREENHOUSE LIGHTING **43**

GREENHOUSE SHELVING AND WORK SPACE **45**

WATERING SYSTEMS **46**
    DRIP IRRIGATION 47
    MAT WATERING 47
    MISTING SYSTEMS 48

VENTILATION **49**

USING YOUR GREENHOUSE **50**
    MISCELLANEOUS TIPS 52

ABOUT THE AUTHOR **55**
    More by Nicolette Goff: *55*

Introduction

Are you concerned about the nutritional value of the produce that's available in your grocery store? Are you aware possible dangers of GMO seeds and produce, and pesticide-laden vegetables and fruits?

Do you wonder whether vegetables and fruits grown thousands of miles away, often picked before they're mature so they don't spoil in transit, have any food value at all?

Today, more and more people are planting gardens and growing at least some of their own food. Gardening is one of the most popular hobbies or activities, and its popularity is growing in leaps and bounds. Urban gardens and community gardens are visible in many cities, creating lush green oases in parks and once-empty lots.

On summer and fall weekends, farmers markets overflow with organic produce, freshly harvested that morning. In other stalls, growers sell their homemade jams, jellies, vinegars and condiments made from their own garden produce.

Are there ways that will allow you to successfully grow your own vegetables, no matter where you live? Can you overcome climate problems like cold, excess rain or high winds, so your plants thrive and produce healthful organic foods for your table?

The answer is yes.

The idea of growing our own food all year round has inspired gardeners' imaginations for centuries. Creative gardeners and farmers in moderate to cool climates have invented different types of shelters to protect their plants and to extend the growing season beyond nature's limitations.

Historical records show the Romans, as early as 20BC, found a way to protect their more tender plants from cold. They dug a pit and erected slabs of rock to line it and to deflect winds, protecting the plants they grew within. These were among the first primitive plant shelters.

Warmed by the sun, the rock slabs radiated the stored solar energy, keeping plants warm after dark. Since glass was not yet invented, sheets of specularium – waxed or oiled canvas – were used as a covering.

In Europe, gardeners have benefited from using different methods of covering their plants for centuries.

Because food, herbs and flowers that are grown out of season have high market value and can demand high prices, there has been a lot of incentive to master methods of growing crops under cover.

Inventive growers, home handymen and gardeners continually work to improve and expand the techniques and structures for growing plants in almost any climate or weather conditions. New materials like fiberglass, plastic and PVC have exploded the possibilities.

Today, back yard gardeners, farmers and commercial growers use a variety of plant covers; from those as elaborate as heated glass greenhouses that cover acres to ones as simple as a plastic bag supported over a single plant.

All these methods are designed to protect plants from the elements, from pests and disease, and to extend the growing season beyond that previously thought possible.

Gardening under cover, regardless of the type or size of shelter, offers protection and encourages healthy plant growth in four different ways:

- **Trapping heat with the greenhouse effect.** The sun's rays radiant energy becomes heat energy when it strikes the soil under the cover. Trapping this energy or warmth accelerates the growth of the plants.
- **Protection from damaging rain.** Heavy spring rains compact the soil surface, wash seeds out of the soil, and destroy young plants. Wet conditions also encourage rot and disease. Covers will deflect the damaging rain.
- **Protection from frost.** As the sun goes down, the heated soil warms the air inside the covered space. By covering plants in early spring and late fall, you protect the plants from freezing and extend the growing season.
- **Protection from wind.** Winds may damage plants by knocking them over or breaking stems. It also chills them, slowing or stunting their growth. The plants under cover are protected from wind forces.

We gardeners are inventive and resourceful people. We have many options when it comes to creating our own unique and useful covers for plants.

Read on to discover some of the most common methods growers and gardeners use as both temporary and permanent covers and shelters for our precious plants.

Temporary Protection with Cloches

"Last night, there came a frost, which has done great damage to my garden.... It is sad that Nature will play such tricks on us poor mortals, inviting us with sunny smiles to confide in her, and then, when we are entirely within her power, striking us to the heart." ~Nathaniel Hawthorne, *The American Notebooks*

Temporary plant shelters or cloches can be almost any size or shape, and were extensively used in the 1800's by French market gardeners. These original cloches were bell-shaped glass covers and each protected a single plant from frost, wind or excessive rain. The word 'cloche' comes from the French word for 'bell'.

I remember my mother using waxed paper domes called Hotkaps to protect her precious tomato plants from late frosts after they had been transplanted into the garden. These are still available, and serve to extend the growing season by 2 to 4 weeks.

A variety of different sized and shaped cloches of either glass or clear plastic similar to the original French glass ones are available through online retailers or at well-stocked garden centers. They are just the right size to protect a single plant.

The Frost Jacket is an innovative cloche to protect your tomato (and other) plants. Made of polypropylene fleece material, these jackets offer protection from frost while the soft material won't cause harm to the buds or leaves. Light and moisture can filter through.

Another efficient way to keep plants from freezing is the Wall of Water – a series of joined tubes of semi-transparent plastic that you fill with water and use to encircle plants. The sun warms the water throughout the day, and heat is radiated to warm the plants as the temperature drops.

Any of these individual cloches will allow you to set out your tender plants from 2 to 4 weeks earlier, giving you a real boost on the growing season.

When frost is in the forecast, just about anything will do for a quick cover up.

Do-it-yourself ideas to make your own temporary cloches:

- Use two recycled windows, forming an inverted vee, to protect several plants at once.

- Drape plastic sheeting, blankets, or old towels over a supporting frame of wood, wire or rigid plastic pipe. Just remember to remove any covers once the chance of freezing has passed.

- Any material that transmits light can be used to make a cloche that stays in place during the day. Other covers, like blankets offer night-time protection, but must be removed during the day.

- Cut the bottom from a gallon plastic container, either of white plastic or clear plastic, and set it over a single plant. The screw top can be removed for ventilation.

Collect your large milk jugs, and you'll have single plant cloches with a convenient handle that you can use over and over!

Cloches that you make yourself have three main advantages:

- They are low cost.

- They are easy to build and move.

- They can be made to specific useful sizes.

Others cloches are more permanent, can cover more than one plant, and are installed in the best possible location to capture the sun's warmth and ward off the cold winds and frosts of spring and fall.

Poly Tunnels – Permanent Cloches

One of the most efficient and useful cloches can be easily made to cover an entire raised planting bed or row of plants. It is a tunnel of poly, supported over your plants on a framework of hoops, and functions as a mini greenhouse.

For more ideas on how others have built and used these cloche tunnels, search online for images of "raised garden bed covers".

Choose the right location for your poly tunnel. If you're installing it over raised beds or in your garden area, the location is already determined.

However, if you have potted plants like tomatoes or peppers that you'd like near your kitchen door, choose somewhere convenient but not too unsightly.

Situate your poly tunnel so that the open end is away from the prevailing winds. Locate it in a protected spot, away from shade trees. Your plants should get as much sun as possible, so an east-west orientation is best.

Choose the strongest, longest-lasting poly you can afford to cover your tunnel. Ideally, it should last for 3 – 5 years. Consider bubble poly, for extra insulation if you live in a colder location or your garden site is exposed.

Wire Mesh Frame Poly Tunnel

Rigid wire mesh is the supporting framework for a covering of poly sheeting.

Purchase a roll of the wire mesh. Six-inch concrete reinforcing mesh is a good choice, stiff and strong. It comes in sheets approximately 2.5 meters by 5 meters (8 feet by 16 feet).

Stucco mesh is more flexible and has holes approximately 2 inches square. You could also use wire garden fencing. Both of these are available in lengths or rolls at home building suppliers or garden supply centers. These types of mesh are more suitable for smaller hoop frame tunnels.

Cut the mesh to size, taking care to cut it in the middle of the wires so you have short prongs to stick into the ground. Form the sections of the mesh you've chosen into arches to cover your row of plants or your raised bed. If you need more than one length, overlap them a few inches. Peg down the edges.

Stretch a sheet of clear plastic film over the top, and weigh it down at the edges with bricks. Alternatively, staple the bottom of the film to a 2X4. Allow the plastic to loosely overlap the ends of your tunnel, so you can open the ends for air circulation.

Raised Bed Hoop Frame Poly Tunnel

If your raised beds are made of wood, then covering the bed with a tunnel cloche is very easy. Here's how to make a permanent and non-disruptive framework for a hoop tunnel. These directions are for a raised bed no more than 42 inches wide.

1. Cut several pieces of half-inch rebar about 2 feet long. Sink them into the ground along the outside of the raised bed frame, placing them 2 feet apart, and opposite one another along the length of the bed.

2. Cut pieces of one inch black PVC tubing, 8 feet long, and slip the hose over the rebar to form hoops across the width of the bed. If your beds are wider than 42 inches, you will need to cut them longer – 10 feet should be sufficient.

3. Stretch plastic film over the hoops, and anchor it in place as above, leaving the ends unfastened so that they can be easily opened.

4. Alternatively, attach the film to a 1 x 3 board along the bottom edges. This makes it easy to roll up the sides for daytime venting.

Your plants may not need to be covered during the day if they've been hardened off naturally, providing the temperature is well above freezing.

During the day, simply open the ends or roll up the sides. Lower the plastic film at night to protect from frost or low nighttime temperatures that can slow or stunt the plant growth.

Vary the length of the PVC tubing to make tunnels of different heights. Keep in mind that your plants should not touch the plastic cover.

Portable Lightweight Cloches

If you don't want or need a permanent poly tunnel cloche, you can easily make smaller portable ones to protect specific areas or plants.

The advantage of portable cloches is that you can move them from place to place as needed. When the weather warms, and they're no longer needed, then you can store them away.

Here is how to make a lightweight portable domed cloche that is both economical and reusable. This type of cloche can be any size you choose, but here is a very versatile one:

- Make a rectangular frame from 2 X 4 lumber, 4 feet by 4 feet, screwed and braced on the 4 corners.

- Drill a 1-inch hole in each corner, but not all the way through.

- Insert two lengths of flexible ¾ PVC pipe into the corner holes, and across diagonally, so they form an arched framework crossing in the center, much like a domed tent frame.

- Put a snap tie around the cross to keep it rigid.

- Lay a 6 mm poly sheet over the framework, and staple it snugly to the 2X4, along the two opposite sides first.

- Snug and staple it along the other two sides. Fold over the excess at the corners, sort of like how you gift-wrap a box.

- Once you've stapled the plastic to the wood frame, cover the staples with duct tape to prevent them from rusting. Trim off any excess plastic from the bottom.

This lightweight cloche can be set over a raised bed, over a grouping of plants, or even over a freshly seeded area. It is easy to lift off for watering and weeding. Lift and support one side up for ventilation. Alternatively, cut holes along the bottom of the plastic for ventilation.

Build at least one dome cloche, and use your ingenuity to design and create other sizes to fit your needs. With just a little expense and a bit of carpentry skill, you can add weeks to your gardening pleasure.

Row Covers – a Modern Invention

Floating row covers were introduced to the gardening community several years ago, and are one of the simplest and easiest products to use to protect your plants.

They are lightweight sheets of polyester or polypropylene – lightweight enough to literally float over the rows of plants. Row covers come in long sheets, up to 100 feet long by 5 to 10 feet wide, so you can cover a whole row with a single one.

Because they're porous, rain can pass through them, and air can circulate more easily. Enough sunlight penetrates so that you can leave the covers on all day. They will ward off up to 3 degrees Fahrenheit of frost, or for more protection as the seasons cool, use a double layer.

Once you've covered your rows of plants in the garden, anchor the cover to the ground on both sides with stones, bricks or blocks of wood, or bank soil along the edges. This will stop them from blowing off in wind, and it will also allow more of the heat to be retained.

Although the light row covers will float above plants without damaging them, they can also be set over wire or PVC hoops to form a tunnel cloche over a row or a raised bed.

Heavier weight row covers protect young seedlings and tender plants from freezing down to 24 degrees F, while allowing 50% of the sun's warming rays through.

Use floating covers to extend the late harvest of fall crops of lettuce, chard, broccoli and spinach by several weeks. Placed over root crops, they delay the freezing of soil so you can harvest carrots, turnips and parsnips well into the colder months.

Cold Frames and Hot Beds

Cold frame greenhouses, cold frames, sun boxes, hotbeds -- call them what you will. Unlike cloches, these are permanent structures, but easily movable. They are generally fairly small, easy to build and extremely useful.

These small structures are designed to give you inexpensive and simple ways to extend your growing season and prevent weather from wiping out your crops. Gardeners in cool or moderate climates have used them universally for centuries.

Once thought of as the poor man's greenhouse, these small grow boxes are a versatile addition to your garden whether or not you have a greenhouse.

In spring, when weather keeps us out of the garden, and we urgently want to get out there and grow things, cold frames are just the thing to keep our thumbs green!

Cold frames use solar energy and insulation to create microclimates for growing plants. How would you like to harvest and eat your own fresh greens in February, or pick blossoms long after frost in the fall? These simple structures allow you to do this.

Let's have a look at the similarities and differences between cold frames and hot beds.

Cold Frames

A cold frame, sometimes called a sun box, is very basic. It is an excellent place to harden off greenhouse grown plants before you plant them out, to start seedlings, to plant fall greens, and to protect potted plants.

It is simply a bottomless wooden box with a lid that lets in light; either placed on the ground or sunk into the ground a few inches. In a sunken cold frame, the earth will act as insulation, and depend solely on the sun's radiation for heat.

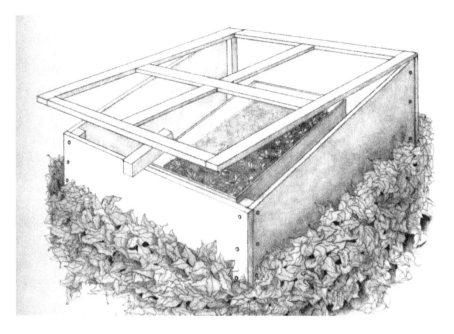

The size is optional, but make sure you can easily reach everything inside. The most useful common size is 3 x 6 feet, but you can make yours as long as you choose. Many gardeners and growers use extended cold frames several feet long. Keep the width to no more than 3 feet, so you can reach everything inside.

The box is generally made of wood, which is a fairly good insulator. Two-inch lumber is better than thinner wood, with more insulation potential. The frame sides can be screwed, bolted or nailed together. The frame should be 8 to 12 inches high in the front, and angle to a height of 14 to 18 inches in the back – a six inch difference.

If you want a more solid enclosure, reinforce the inside corners with 2 x 2 supports. Alternatively, brace the frame on the outside with 1 x 3 boards nailed to the corners.

The most essential part of a cold frame is the slanting roof. It is always a transparent or semi-transparent material that transmits heat from the sun. Old sash windows work well as covers, and if you use these, you'll have to build the cold frame to fit them.

The cover can be made from rigid or flexible plastic sheets in a wood framework. You may need to add additional support for plastic covers, and two-inch strips of wood nailed across the frame will do the job.

Make the lid a bit larger than the size of the frame so water drains off the front edge, not into the wood of the frame. Hinge the lid to the back of the frame, and devise a way to secure it from blowing closed. Make the cover easily movable and adjustable for ventilation.

Both cold frames and sun boxes rely solely on the sun (that's why they're called sun boxes) for their warming ability, so place them in a sunny but sheltered spot, one that's protected from wind chill.

Locate a cold frame with the tall side against or in the shelter of a wall, hedge, or compost bin. This will be the north side, positioned so the frame is angled to catch the sun's rays.

You could also use stone, brick or concrete blocks for the frame. These are more durable (and more permanent) than wood, and retain more heat. It's simple to sink this type a few inches into the ground so frost won't cause movement as the ground freezes and thaws.

Set the cold frame in the best location, and dig out 3 to 4 inches of the soil inside the frame. Replace it with gravel for drainage. If you plan to plant directly into the cold frame, top it with 6 inches of good loam mixed with compost. A second frame without the addition of planting soil can be put to use to shelter potted plants.

Use your cold frames for starting hardy annuals and early salad greens. Keep in mind that seed germination is sensitive to cold so choose to seed those that will germinate in lower temperatures. To eliminate any shock to the seeds, place the cold frame in a sunny location a couple of weeks before you want to seed. That way, the soil inside will have the chance to warm up.

Ensure the soil is evenly moist when starting seeds, as it will dry out more quickly inside the protected warmth of the cold frame. Once germination occurs, vent the cold frame during the day to disperse heat and to allow air circulation. Good air circulation is critical to prevent damping off of your seedlings.

A cold frame is also a good spot to harden off potted seedlings before they are planted in the garden. You eliminate transplanting shock, since the plants can be slowly acclimated.

In general, wait until seedlings have formed multiple sets of true leaves and are well rooted before moving them into cold frames. Set the potted up plants closely together in the cold frame and start by venting the frame during the warmest part of the day. Gradually increase the length of time the frame is left open.

Word of warning:

On a clear sunny spring day, the inside temperature can zoom up to 90F degrees very quickly. A rule of thumb is when the outdoor temperature reaches 40F, open the frame 6 inches, and if it reaches 50F, then open it completely. Close the cover by mid-afternoon to retain heat over night.

On cold nights, plants in the cold frame may need some extra protection. Heat escapes readily through glass, so prevent them from being chilled or frozen by adding insulation on top of the cover. Old blankets, straw, pieces of lumber or dry leaves in a sack will do. You can also bank up straw or leaves around the wood sides of the frame.

Remember to uncover the cold frame during the day.

Your cold frame can be put to work all year round. In spring, it will be a warmer place to start your cold weather plants like parsley, chives and lettuce, as well as hardy annuals.

In summer, place houseplants in it and use a shade cover to protect them from sun. It is a perfect spot to root cuttings of your perennials, start biennials or winter crops.

Sow cold-weather crops in the frames in late summer. Cool season greens such as spinach, lettuce, Belgian endive, kale, broccoli and Swiss chard are good choices. Choose cultivars that are more cold tolerant, water and fertilize them generously in the fall.

As winter approaches, water them sparingly and mulch around the plants with straw or dry leaves. Add extra insulation to the outside of your cold frame and cover the top at night, and you can enjoy fresh greens well into fall, and even through a mild winter.

Hot Beds

A hot bed is simply a cold frame with a source of heat inside it. It can be a thermostatically controlled electric heating cable, an incandescent light bulb or even fresh manure!

Any of these heating methods will keep plants from freezing even when outside temperatures dip as low as 15°F.

To install a heating cable, dig out about 6 inches of soil and lay down the cable, looping it back and forth. Distribute the cable uniformly throughout the bed. Irregular spacing makes temperature control difficult. Generally, a 60-foot cable should heat about 36 square feet of bed area.

Cover the heating cable with about 2 inches of sand, then wire mesh for protection. Top it with 4 inches of soil. This warms the plants from the bottom up – warming the soil first, and then the air inside the frame.

Suspend 25-watt incandescent bulbs along the inside of the cover, and connect them to a power source and a timer. Four 25-watt bulbs are adequate for a 3 x 6 foot frame if spaced around the sides. Use waterproof wiring and sockets.

This method warms the air inside the frame, but does not do much to warm the soil. It's less effective than a heating cable, but easier and less expensive to install.

These 2 methods both depend on an easily accessible source of electricity, but there is another more 'natural' way to make a hot bed - using fresh manure.

Natural Hot Bed

Did you know that as manure composts, it emits heat!

To heat a hotbed with fresh manure, first dig out an area the size of the frame about 12 inches deep. Fill it completely with fresh – not dried - manure mixed with an equal quantity of straw or dry leaves. The straw or leaves adds carbon content, as well as aerating the pile.

Cover the manure with poly, and leave it for 4 days. After another 4 days, turn it with a fork or shovel to release some of the heat and move the cool edges into the center. Leave it another 4 days. By now, composting should be well under way.

Remove the poly and replace the frame of your hot bed around the pit of composting manure. Add about 2 inches of sand and 4 inches of garden soil, leaving room for plants.

It may be more convenient to sow seeds in flats or pots, and place them in the hotbed. In this case, the soil layer is not essential and the flats or pots are placed on the sand.

Wait a couple of days before you plant into your new naturally heated hotbed, so that heat can build up within it. You will have 3 to 4 weeks of extra heat as the manure mixture continues to decompose.

And at the end of the season, dig out the manure/compost, and add it to your compost pile, or spread it on your garden.

Overwintering Plants in a Cold Frame

A sunken cold frame or a hot frame can provide a place to overwinter semi-tender plants. Either will give you the right conditions to keep your plants in a secure dormancy, ready to resume growth in the spring.

Build a sunken frame by digging a square or rectangular hole in a spot away from wind. Line the hole with bricks or concrete block pavers, and prepare a rigid white plastic cover that can be lifted for venting.

How to prepare less hardy perennial plants for overwintering:

- Cut your plants back as much as possible before fall frosts arrive.

- Place each plant into a large pot, with plenty of soil to insulate the root mass.

- If you have several plants to overwinter, pack them closely together in the cold frame. Water them well.

- Add leaves, straw or mulch over the plants and soil, filling in any gaps.

- Cover the frame with a white plastic cover to minimize the amount of sunlight entering, and to keep the temperature inside the frame from rising too high. If it gets too warm the plants may start growing.

- You may need to vent the frame during the sunny days to prevent overheating. Depending on the winter weather, you can also insulate the frame by banking up leaves or straw around it, and covering the top at night.

A similar method to overwintering plants in cold frames is to create a rectangle of six straw bales. Set the bales two on each side, and one bale between them at each end so that there is a center square opening the width and length of the bale – usually 30 or 36 inches.

Place the prepared potted plants in the center, surround them with loose straw, and cover the opening as above, with a white plastic sheet.

Come spring, you can break up the straw bales and use the straw as mulch. It's also a good source of carbon to build up your compost!

Cold Frame Greenhouses

A cold frame greenhouse is a **miniature greenhouse**, and many kinds are available on the market. It is easy to construct your own.

They are generally taller than cold frames, standing up to 3 feet tall. A framework of wood, metal or rigid plastic supports the sides that are made with a semi-transparent polycarbonate plastic rigid sheet that can be double-walled for insulation.

The roof is transparent, slanted and hinged. It can open from either one side or the center/top so it can be accessed from either side and held open for releasing excessive heat.

 Durable, rigid and lightweight, these small greenhouses are easily moved around in the garden where they're needed, or positioned to catch the best sun.

Use these mini greenhouse style frames to protect potted plants, to harden off seedlings or to grow early or late crops of greens and other small vegetables.

Any of the methods and structures we've discussed so far can extend the growing season and to provide a protected environment for your plants.

Why not add a couple of cold frames or a small cold frame greenhouse to your yard, and enjoy those early spring salads, fresh from your own garden!

Portable Mini Greenhouses

Full-sized greenhouses can be quite expensive, and costly to maintain. It is often impractical for home gardeners to build or buy one. If you are short on space, one of these mini greenhouses can serve you well.

Portable greenhouses now are readily available for use in the garden, on a patio, or even on a balcony. These small light structures are ideal for starting the growing season early, and extending it in the fall. They are also useful for overwintering hardier perennial potted plants.

Because they are portable, these greenhouses are lightweight and compact – easy to set up or transport. They can be stored in any convenient space – a garage, garden shed or even a closet – during the coldest season.

Why would you consider a portable mini greenhouse?

Many gardeners don't really need a greenhouse all year round. A mini one is ideal for their needs. For others, using one of these small structures gives the feel of a real greenhouse, perhaps leading them to build or buy a full sized permanent one.

Portable greenhouses are ideal for early seed starting, protecting tender plants in the shoulder seasons, rooting cuttings, and overwintering hardy perennials or winter vegetables.

On a balcony or patio, they are useful for growing greens, herbs and small vegetables. Useful also for houseplants, this mini greenhouse is a protected spot for giving them a summer outdoors. Just like the full-sized kinds, these trap heat from the sun, retain moisture and offer protection from the weather and from pests.

A sturdy rust-resistant frame supports the covering of UV protected translucent fabric/plastic. A zippered front rolls up for easy access. Some even have a roll-up side window for climate control, equipped with netting to control pests or insects.

Portable mini greenhouses are commercially available in a variety of sizes and shapes. Some are so small they will hold only a couple of shelves and plants, while others are up to six feet square, with four or five shelves on either side for plants.

Another style has a wood framework and shelves, with sides and top of single or twin-walled rigid polycarbonate sheets. These are sturdier and heavier, so less susceptible to strong winds. The polycarbonate sheets are stronger than glass and a better insulator than poly sheeting.

Some are designed to be freestanding, while others are made to set against a wall. The lean-to types use the wall for protection and shelter, as well as a heat sink.

If you plan on using a greenhouse only to grow a few plants, to germinate seeds or to protect a few plants over the winter, then a portable greenhouse may be all you need. Maintaining a small greenhouse is much less expensive than a full sized one.

A mini greenhouse can be a good investment for any gardener, and a useful supplement for a gardener with a larger greenhouse.

Sun Pit Solar Greenhouse

f you live in an area with lots of sunny and clear days, then a sun pit solar greenhouse could be just the ticket to becoming more self-sufficient. These are built like very large and permanent hot frames, sunk into the ground, with a sloped transparent cover.

A sun pit greenhouse takes advantage of the earth's natural insulation as well as solar energy to create a warm growing space. Four to six feet into the ground, the temperatures will remain about 50°F – warmer in winter and cooler in summer.

Properly designed, it naturally emits warmth at night from four sides and the floor. In an above ground greenhouse, only one side - the floor - is heated during the day and radiates that heat at night.

Choose a location that drains well, since you don't want to be working in a muddy or water filled space. A sloping site is perfect.

A pit greenhouse has walls below ground level, with the roof sited above ground. The roof can be arched, A-frame, shed or rounded. The simplest choice is either an arched or a shed roof.

An arched or rounded roof will give you the most interior space for plants. A shed roof gives you ample light, and the back wall - a good 4 to 6 feet above ground - can be an added heat sink. Situate the length of the roof facing south to collect the most solar energy.

Interested in a solar sun pit greenhouse? Visit online at http://www.inspirationgreen.com/pit-greenhouses.html for a collection of photos showing various sun pit constructions around the world, as well as several good references to study.

Constructing a Sun Pit Greenhouse

Save your back, and rent a backhoe to excavate a space four feet deep and no smaller than eight feet by twelve feet. Larger sun pits will keep a much more stable inside temperature.

Dig a sump in the pit's floor, about 30 inches deep and line it with bricks. This is available for any irrigation water or seepage to collect in. It can be pumped out if it doesn't drain.

Square the sides of the excavation, line it with heavy 6-mil poly, and make a concrete footing around the circumference. Build a block wall atop it. This wall should be a foot higher than the surrounding ground in front and at least 8 feet high in the back. Design it so that the glassed roof will be at 90° to the solstice sun, for maximum sun exposure.

At this point, level the floor and either lay pavers on a bed of sand or spread 4 inches of pea gravel. Plan the entry and stairs at one end.

The apex of the roof, if you plan an arched roof, should be at 10 feet above the floor. One end wall will have the entry door, and the other should have venting. A large pit will require extra venting in the roof.

The north facing side of an arched or peaked roof can be solid and insulated, while the south facing side will be either glass or fitted fiberglass panels, sealed and weatherproof.

Now you're ready to add staging for your plants!

Sunk into the ground, a well-built sun pit solar greenhouse takes advantage of both the sun's energy and the natural insulation of the earth. Carefully managed, it is a successful and practical alternative solar greenhouse.

A Short History of Greenhouses

The first examples of practical greenhouses (sometimes called glass houses) using glass date to around 1300AD. Most of these had one wall of glass, since it was both hard to make and expensive. These structures were built to protect and grow exotic and tender plants like oranges, pineapples, and other fruits.

Early glass houses were designed to capture and retain heat from the sun but were not very efficient. They had virtually no way to control heat build-up during the day. At night, they needed to be closed up and protected to prevent freezing.

As time went on, the efficiency of these glass houses was improved by incorporating angled glass walls, methods of ventilation, and installing heating flues.

In the mid 1800's when plate glass became more common and less expensive, and glass taxes were abolished in Europe, the design and popularity of greenhouses started to change.

Wealthy landowners competed in building elaborate structures to grow and display exotic flowers and fruits. For years, greenhouses were the monopoly of Europe's aristocratic classes or universities.

At that time, the moneyed aristocrats often imported rare and exotic plants from foreign countries and built enormous glass houses, called 'conservatories' to protect them. They created botanical gardens with a greenhouse at the core, and many of these beautiful gardens are still attractions today.

Two important innovations in the 1800's gave greenhouse design a quantum leap forward. They were the design of a curved roof instead of a flat one, allowing higher concentrations of the sun's rays to enter; and the use of iron instead of wood as the framework. This allowed greenhouses to be structurally stronger, larger and capable of absorbing more light.

 In Britain, Joseph Paxton, a horticulturist, introduced many changes to the greenhouse design concept. A gardener for large estates in England, Paxton initiated greenhouse design and construction.

He built a greenhouse for the sole purpose of housing and preserving just one plant – the giant Victoria Regia lily.

The Duke of Devonshire at that time brought the flower to England to propagate it and gift to Queen Victoria. In the controlled greenhouse that Paxton built, the plant produced 126 blooms during the following year.

He was famous for designing and building the Palm House at Kew Gardens in 1842. It measured 370 feet (110 m) long, 100 feet (30 m) wide and over 66 feet (20 m) high.

Nine years later, he designed and built his masterpiece - the famous Crystal Palace in London - to house the Great Exhibition of 1851. All of his amazing glass structures were possible because of the availability of cast iron and plate glass.

The Crystal Palace, built in Hyde Park in 1851, had 990,000 square feet of display area, and was 1,851 feet (564 m) long, with an interior height of 128 feet (39 m). It had the largest amount of glass ever seen at one time, and needed no interior lighting!

After the exhibition, this enormous glass house was dismantled and moved to an area in south London, where it stood from 1854 until it burned down in 1936.

It is easy to imagine how Joseph Paxton must have felt fulfilled with his life. His Crystal Palace has been acclaimed by many as a piece of architectural art that was unsurpassed in its day.

"Who loves a garden loves a greenhouse too." William Cowper

Greenhouses Today

With today's growing concern about the quality of the food, many are growing vegetables and fruits in a variety of places and with a variety of methods. Back yard gardens and community gardens are springing up.

Ideally, most people would like a steady supply of locally grown organic food. And what better control can you have over the quality of your food than actually growing your own?

The idea of building a greenhouse is just one step toward gaining self-sufficiency and growing healthier food. However, it may not be just a constant supply of healthy fruits or vegetables that makes us decide to invest in a greenhouse.

Most greenhouse owners are familiar with the concept of prolonging the growing season to grow their own plants and flowers. Others have seen the opportunity to use it for heating their home.

Building and growing both food and ornamental plants within a greenhouse can be sources of pure enjoyment, learning and fun for everyone in the family.

Greenhouses come in all shapes, styles and sizes, and range from affordable to very expensive. You can build your own greenhouse by using plastic film stretched over a home-made structure such as a hoop house, or purchase elaborate metal and glass pre-manufactured glass houses.

A greenhouse, a glasshouse, a conservatory or a hothouse - they're all structures where plants – fruits, vegetables, flowers, vines and trees – are grown. They have translucent or transparent walls and roof, staging inside for plantings, and possibly a source of heat and irrigation.

They're strategically located so that the sun's energy is best captured to warm the plants, soil and other components inside the greenhouse.

Regardless of the choice, each of these structures will give you the ability to extend the growing season beyond that which nature has dictated, and give you pleasure and relaxation while working with plants.

How Does a Greenhouse Capture Heat?

The glass (or fiberglass or plastic covering) of a greenhouse allows the sun's energy or radiation to be transmitted within the structure, and traps that energy in the form of heat.

The heat warms the plants and other surfaces, including the ground or floor inside the greenhouse. This warmed base or floor also warms the air near the ground, and radiates heat over time.

A small window or vent near the roof of a greenhouse to get rid of excess heat is necessary. Most commercial greenhouses have an automatic cooling system triggered to open and close by pre-set temperature gauges. An auto vent maintains a range of temperatures inside automatically.

Benefits of a Greenhouse

Primarily, a greenhouse gives the gardener a large and permanent structure with the ability to extend the growing season at both ends of the season. Early vegetables can be planted indoors in a protective climate, and then transplanted when they mature.

A greenhouse owner thus can gain several weeks to the growing season, especially if the greenhouse is heated.

In addition, mature but tender plants such as tomatoes, peppers, melons and cucumbers will bear their fruit well into the fall if they're protected from cold in a greenhouse environment.

Just imagine – juicy red tomatoes just off the vine in October or November!

Within a greenhouse, you have control of temperature, light and moisture, so that you can, with experience, obtain guaranteed results. Within the closed environment, it is easier to control possible insect and pest infestations or plant diseases.

As well, many plant varieties thrive best in a warm, moist climate that can easily be duplicated in a greenhouse.

In addition some gardeners choose to specialize with one species of fruit, vegetable or flowering plant. For example, some have built greenhouses for the sole purpose of growing and preserving their orchids. Others grow tender vegetables like tomatoes, peppers and cucumbers, or enjoy fresh salad greens year round.

Even if you have limited space in your yard, you can enjoy a greenhouse. Freestanding greenhouses that take just a few square feet of space can be installed on decks, balconies or even rooftops.

A greenhouse offers easy access by the elderly and disabled, since greenhouses are less physically demanding than working in gardens and plants are generally raised above ground level.

Greenhouse owners can also reduce gardening costs by growing and propagating their own bedding plants, herbs and vegetables rather than buying expensive starter plants.

And finally, a greenhouse can become an escape or refuge, a place to work and relax within a natural environment.

Types of Greenhouses

Once you've decided that you want to build a greenhouse, the next decision is what type and size to build. If you know what kinds of plants you want to grow, that will help in making the right choice.

Questions to consider:

How will I use my greenhouse?

What size greenhouse will suit me (and my location) best?

Am I concerned about safety glazing to protect children and dogs?

Do I want a free-standing or attached greenhouse?

Do I want my greenhouse to be the main feature in my garden?

Is my yard exposed to strong winds or much shade?

Factors such as cost and available space will determine the type of greenhouse you build. Begin by researching online and if possible, visiting some greenhouse suppliers to look at the various models.

Ask questions and get all of them answered before you make a final decision on the type of greenhouse that is best for you.

Deciding on Your Greenhouse

Several factors can come into play in deciding on the kind of greenhouse you will buy or build. The desired temperature of the greenhouse, the structural design and the most suitable construction materials will all come into play.

Temperature Factor

The desirable temperature may be the main factor in choosing your greenhouse, because of the plant varieties you want to grow. The climate zone you live in is also important when deciding on the kind of greenhouse that will suit you best.

There are three types of greenhouses in terms of temperature control: warm greenhouses, cool greenhouses and cold greenhouses.

Warm Greenhouse

A **warm greenhouse's** inside temperature is maintained at a minimum of 55 degrees Fahrenheit (13 degrees Celsius). Choose this type if you plan to grow plants all year round, including exotic flowers and fruits.

Heating and lighting equipment must be installed to meet the growth requirements of any tropical and exotic plant species you decide to grow.

A warm greenhouse can be an expensive proposition, as fuel costs will be about 3 times higher than a cool greenhouse.

Cool Greenhouse

The temperature inside a **cool greenhouse** is generally kept above 45 degrees Fahrenheit (7 degrees Celsius). Both heat and light require supplementing during the cool months. The plants inside are protected from wind, rain, snow and frost.

In a cool greenhouse, you can grow a larger variety of plants, perhaps as many as you would in an outdoor garden.

Growth here is 3 to 4 weeks ahead of a cold greenhouse. This is a great place to start less hardy bedding plants, and to over-winter frost-sensitive perennials.

Cold Greenhouse

A cold greenhouse is heated only by the sun. Plants are protected from rain, wind and snow, but not frost. Growth will be three to four weeks ahead of outdoor plants, growing time is extended similarly in the fall for potted plants.

It is a great place for starting your plants and vegetables that you'll move later into the garden. Generally it's only used seasonally, and is not suitable for overwintering plants except in mild climates.

Structural Design Factors

There are also different types of greenhouses based on structural design. There are three structural types:

1. Lean-To

The lean-to type of greenhouse is rarely used for commercial purposes because of size restrictions, but is popular among hobbyists or homeowners.

 It is best located on a south or west facing existing wall of the house or a garage. Lean-tos can be built angled or straight sided, with a flat roof or a curved top. Many lean-to greenhouses are available commercially, ranging from widths as small as 2 feet to those 10 feet wide.

Homeowners often build this type of greenhouse as a sunroom addition, giving them a four-season area to enjoy the views and outdoor surroundings, as well as enjoying its passive heating.

2. Detached

Detached greenhouses – as the name suggests – are independent stand-alone structures.

One type is the **Quonset,** built from arched metal rafters and with short walls. Either polyethylene or polycarbonate is used as the covering, forming a strong tunnel-like structure.

Each end is closed, with ventilation and doors placed at the ends. It is one of the most common types for commercial food production. Smaller Quonset style greenhouses, often molded in one piece, are available for home gardeners.

Hoop houses are similar in style to Quonsets, and are very easy for homeowners to build. They consist of a frame of shaped tubular pipe, covered with sturdy polyethylene film. The two ends generally are fitted with either doors or a door and window for access and ventilation.

Build your own hoop greenhouses in whatever size is best suited to your space. Any size is possible, from a small tunnel that covers one row or a raised bed to a large one that can support tall plants and shelving along the sides.

Hoop houses are low cost alternative structures, often used as a way of economizing or as temporary greenhouses. They generally require recovering with plastic every 3-4 years. They are similar to poly tunnels described previously, but are larger, taller and more permanent structures.

3. Even Span Greenhouse

This type of structure is the most familiar greenhouse. Built as detached structures, the roof has an even pitch and an even width. It's shaped like a simple house with straight sides and two gable ends.

The framework can be wood, aluminum or steel. The covering is either permanent or semi-permanent material like glass or rigid plastic sheets.

If you build your own framework with wood, cover it with sheets of the strongest poly film available, stapled onto the frame. Cover the lines of staples with laths to prevent tearing and leaking. Expect up to 8 years before this type of covering needs replacing.

Material Factors

A third way of looking at greenhouse types is the material they incorporate as the covering or skin - glass, fiberglass, or plastic. Each type has its advantages and disadvantages.

1. Glass

Glass type greenhouses are the most traditional. They may be constructed with slanted sides, straight sides, curves and eaves. Aluminum-framed glass buildings are low maintenance and have clean lines and a weather-tight structure.

Pre-fabricated kits for glass greenhouse kits are available in many models and sizes. Vents, doors, windows and staging for plants are usually included and are easily mounted.

The two disadvantages of glass are its fragility and high cost.

2. Fiberglass

Fiberglass greenhouses are molded and shaped in one self-supporting piece, so there is nothing to assemble. They are stronger than wood, and will not rust. UV protection is integrated into the resins so that they will not deteriorate from sunlight.

They are light, strong and hail-proof. However, lower quality fiberglass will discolor over time, reducing the amount of sunlight and heat that can penetrate. If you decide to go for fiberglass, choose the highest quality grade, as it will save you money in the long run.

Corrugated fiberglass panels can be used as the skin for a framed greenhouse, either for the walls or the roof. They are strong, rigid and can easily be cut to size.

3. Plastic

Plastic as a greenhouse skin is becoming very popular. It is low cost, less liable to breaking or damage than glass, and will allow in enough heat for most plants. Many smaller portable greenhouses made of plastic are available on the market today, suitable for patios and even balcony gardening.

Your best choices in plastic for greenhouses are polyethylene (poly film) and polycarbonate.

Polyethylene sheeting is lightweight and inexpensive as a cover material. It stands up well during the in fall, winter and spring, but will start deteriorate during the summer with constant exposure to the sun's ultraviolet rays.

Look for UV-inhibited polyethylene, which is available in six-millimeter thickness, in rolls up to 40 feet wide and 100 feet long. It's carried in all building supply stores.

Used more and more, polycarbonate panels are rigid, light and tough. They are strong enough to be used for roofs, providing there is adequate infrastructure. The unique "double wall" cellular structure keeps heat from escaping while it transmits 80% of the available light.

Polyvinyl chloride or PVC tubing and fittings (available from plumbing suppliers and in building centers) are simple to put together as a framework for a poly film covering. This is a great way to frame your own greenhouse. Frames made of PVC piping, when properly installed, can last many years.

Combinations of these styles, frameworks and coverings are as unlimited as your own imagination.

My personal home handyman built my 8 X 12 greenhouse with a frame of fir 2 x 4's, on a foundation of 6 x 6 fir beams laid a gravel floor.

We designed it in the even span style, with a mansard roof. The walls were 6 feet high, and the mansard shape of the roof helped create even more head space.

We roofed it with panels of translucent corrugated fiberglass, and covered the sides and ends with 6 mil polyethylene. It had good access and ventilation with a door at one end and a window in the other.

Siting the Greenhouse

Site a freestanding structure well away from fences, hedges and buildings that can shade out the sun. However, a windbreak of a tall fence or hedge on the north and east sides will offer wind protection and lower heating bills.

Your new greenhouse should be set well away from trees – 30 feet is recommended. Overhanging branches will not only shade, but also will drop leaves, seeds and dirt; and branches that break off in high wind are a potential hazard.

Locate the foundation on level ground situated so that the roof ridge will run from east to west to catch the best sun. With a lean-to, the best site is a west wall. A south wall can be a sun trap – fine in cooler months, but much too hot for your plants in summer unless you have adequate vent openings.

It's also important to avoid areas where the ground is waterlogged, or in dips that hold frost. Build a strong and level foundation – either well-packed and drained gravel, pressure treated timbers, or a concrete slab. Ensure good drainage in the floor, grading the site if necessary.

If you have not poured a concrete slab, you will need a walkway down the center. Lay down 4 inches of tamped sand, and lay unmortared bricks or a duckboard over it. Frame the brick walkway with treated 2X4 lumber. Finish the remainder of the floor with a layer of pea gravel so containers can drain.

Locate your greenhouse as close to a source of water and power as possible, and also close to your garden plot. It should be easy to get to for loading and unloading supplies from a vehicle.

Remember – a greenhouse is hard to move once it is set up, so take time to site it in the best possible location.

Essential Tools and Materials

Once you've answered the initial questions, and chosen the best style and size of greenhouse for your personal circumstances, you're ready to consider what goes inside it.

All the materials for planting, growing, and maintaining your plants, along with the necessary tools should be in place before you even think about sowing seeds or buying plants.

Begin with the soil.

Compost, potting or garden soil, peat or coir and some sand or perlite are all necessary. Buy a good-sized bin to mix your own combination of potting soil, depending on what you're growing. Different plants have different requirements. Garbage cans with lids make good storage bins for your mixed soils.

Keep the black plastic flats that nurseries use to display their plants. They are useful for starting seeds and holding small trays or pots of transplants. You can also build your own flats for starting seeds.

Collect styrofoam cups, empty plastic containers, and milk cartons or buy small plastic plant pots. Seeds sprout quickly and once they grow large enough to move into separate containers, they can be gently lifted and transferred into these containers. Recycled containers are inexpensive and can be washed and re-used.

Keep any of the plastic pots that have held nursery plants, from the small ones to the very large ones. Wash them out and stack them to use as you pot up plants. The largest ones, for example, can be used for individual tomato plants, which can be moved outdoors in summer and inside the greenhouse as the weather cools.

Stockpile broken clay pots, pebbles, charcoal or gravel and place these in the bottom of your pots for proper drainage. Be sure to soak clay pots in water a few minutes before using them. This will prevent the clay pot from absorbing the moisture from the potting soil.

A plant propagator is a necessity if you're planning to start your own plants. Some seeds, like cucumbers and tomatoes, need a temperature of 60 to 75 degrees F to germinate properly.

A **heated propagating tray** is the best answer. It is a plastic container with a raised transparent cover and a built-in heating element in the tray. Choose one that uses electricity and has a thermostatic control. The cover should have one or more ventilators in the top. It's a mini-greenhouse just for starting seeds!

If you need trellises inside your greenhouse for climbers like beans or cucumbers, you can make them of wire or wood. Alternatively, buy bamboo stakes from your local nursery.

Keep a set of hand gardening tools in the greenhouse, along with sturdy plastic gloves, a pair of secateurs, and an accurate thermometer. I've also found that a large plastic tub to hold water is very handy, to either wash pots or as a reserve for hand watering.

Greenhouse Lighting

If you're only using your greenhouse to start bedding plants, and to extend the growing season by a few weeks, you likely will not need to install a lighting system. **Portable grow lights** can be set up over your bedding plants.

However, if you plan extended season use, some type of supplemental lighting is essential.

Commercial growers in large greenhouses traditionally use high intensity discharge lighting (halide). This broad spectrum lighting adds to natural sunlight, and serves as a substitute during long winters when natural sunlight is in short supply. These lights are energy efficient and operational costs are low.

Today, LED lighting is available for greenhouses and produces larger coverage areas with much higher intensity and deeper penetration than traditional halide lights. They are more expensive to install, but the cost of power used will be considerably less, and they will last much longer.

Broad spectrum grow lights produce many light waves that plants can't use efficiently. LED grow lights can be selected to only deliver the specific colors of light used by plants for efficient and healthy growth.

Use LED grow lamps to extend the day period of your light cycle by 4 to 6 hours during the winter months. This could extend your grow season to 365 days per year!

Both LED and broad spectrum grow lights are much more efficient and closer to natural light than conventional fluorescents

Heating the Greenhouse

An unheated (cold) greenhouse is generally a protected spot to grow more tender crops such as tomatoes and cucumbers in the summer, mums in the fall, and not much use in winter except to over-winter very hardy plants through the colder months.

If you want to extend your growing season and the range of plants you can grow, you'll need some way to heat your greenhouse during colder months. If you've decided on a cool greenhouse, the most common type for home gardeners, then maintain temperatures above 45°F.

Electric heat is the best choice – no fumes and easily controlled. Hire a professional to install any electric heaters. Electric fan heaters are the most common - and best - choice for a small greenhouse. They circulate the air quickly, and some will allow the fan to run even when the heating element is switched off.

Electric heating cables are another option. The most common is the soil heating type, placed in the soil or on staging under the plants. This is a very economical heating method, since you're directing heat exactly where it's required.

Another choice is a fuel stove – wood, natural gas, propane or paraffin. These all require adequate ventilation, and control of the heat is not easy, except in the case of gases.

The only recommended type of fuel is propane, with the bottles placed on a flat firm surface outside the greenhouse. Water vapor and carbon dioxide are both produced as a burn by-product. Be aware that too much water vapor can cause mold to grow.

If you've opted for a lean-to attached to your house or a conservatory/sun room, tap into your in-house heating. However, you'll need a separate thermostat, since house heating may be set too low at night, just when the greenhouse requires added heat.

Greenhouse Shelving and Work Space

A flat workspace is essential for working inside your greenhouse and to maximize and organize your greenhouse space. As your plant varieties grow, you will need adjustable shelves, tables and plant supports.

One popular type of bench that greenhouse hobbyists like is the cedar double layer bench. They are durable and efficient to use.

For shelves, you can opt for two and three section lengths made of aluminum wire or sturdy three quarter inch plywood. Shelves should be a minimum of 12 inches wide, and installed on the north side of the greenhouse to prevent the growing plants from being shaded.

Staging is the term for permanent shelving or counter space. Traditionally, it has a slatted surface so air can circulate around the plants on it. However, this type of surface is not suitable for some watering systems or as a work surface for potting or mixing soils. Solid staging with a shallow lip works well in these circumstances.

A collapsible bench or table makes a useful work space. Grow and pot up bedding plants at a convenient height on it in spring, and then fold it up and store it away in summer to increase your growing space for tomatoes and other plants.

Watering Systems

You installed a faucet within the greenhouse as you constructed it – didn't you? Bury water piping below the frost line, and have an anti-frost faucet fitted.

Since watering your plants is essential (and frequent in a greenhouse), you need an easy-to use and convenient way to water.

If you're just starting to build or set up your greenhouse, now is the time to design a suitable water system. It is much easier to plan faucets and drains before construction begins, rather than trying to find a watering solution later.

Regardless of the type of watering system you use, you should have a floor that drains well. Puddles are unsanitary and dangerous.

There are several types of watering systems that work well in a greenhouse. Each one has specific benefits or weaknesses, so you should explore the options before making an investment.

You can choose either an automatic or hand held watering system to make your watering more efficient, or use a combination of both.

Automatic irrigation systems generally come equipped with an drip irrigation and fertilizer system. Day or night, they regularly water the plants and adjust the flow of fertilizer. Some have a tank in which the water and fertilizer are mixed and distributed to plants via hoses, Y-connections and drip pins.

In a smaller home greenhouse, you may opt not to install a watering system. A watering can lets you satisfy individual water needs the very well, but is only useful for a small collection of plants.

It's easy to connect a hose to an exterior faucet, and bring it inside the greenhouse. Connect it to a greenhouse garden coil **indoor/outdoor-watering wand**.

This is a "self-coiling" hose made of rugged and durable polyurethane tubing. It produces ultra-fine mists and sprays in soft, gentle streams. Some wand models extend to as long as 60 feet. It's no hassle to store it because of its self-coiling mechanism.

Drip Irrigation

Drip irrigation systems have many advantages. They conserve water, since flow is regulated and timed. Many systems are marketed, and they are all very easy to install.

Drip systems consist of many small tubes branching from a PVC hose, and each one delivers water to an individual plant or container. The whole system can be connected to sensors and timers for a completely automated system.

If your greenhouse has beds along the walls, then a perforated or drip hose will also work well. These hoses have tiny holes that allow water to ooze out slowly. The hose is simply laid along plants rows in the bed, and can be connected to a timer for interval watering.

Mat Watering

Mat watering is a good system if you have groupings of plants in various sized pots. A thick mat is placed over poly on the bench, and one end is set into a gutter or container filled with water.

Capillary action keeps the mat wet; and the plant pots, with large perforations on the bottom, take up the water in the same way. Many garden suppliers carry these mats.

Their downside is they will eventually clog with algae and degrade.

Misting Systems

Misting is an efficient way to keep seedlings moist. A pipe with fine nozzles can be set up over a row of plants or seedling trays. The fine spray will not damage tender and new plants. This is an efficient way to keep cuttings that you are propagating moist.

Misters also help maintain humidity through evaporation of the fine spray. In turn, this cools the temperature inside the greenhouse.

However, misting is not a good way to water large plants, since constantly wet foliage encourages mold to grow, and the root systems do not get the deep watering they need.

Misting systems can be set up with electronic timers, programmed to mist throughout the day at set times and for set periods.

As you research watering systems in detail, you may find that a combination of systems will be the best way to go, depending on how you intend to use your greenhouse.

Watering can become a time consuming job in the greenhouse, but the health of your plants depends on it.

Regardless of which system or systems you use, keep a close watch on your plants, and be aware of their water needs at all times.

Ventilation

Adequate ventilation is one of the most vital components in a greenhouse. Without airflow, plants are prone to mold, overheating, and pest infestations. Airflow is also essential for pollination.

Larger greenhouses will need a hinged roof ventilator that opens automatically when the inside temperature rises above 80°F. Most commercially available greenhouse kits come with these automatic ventilators. If you're building your own greenhouse, you can buy these auto-openers and install them on your roof vents or windows.

In larger greenhouses, locate vents near the floor encourage cross ventilation – air enters and flows upward toward the top. This air circulation is the most efficient way to vent excess heat and have sufficient fresh air.

You may need to install a fan in a larger greenhouse to keep the air moving. A constant supply of fresh air (carbon dioxide) is necessary for photosynthesis.

Extra ventilators or windows that open will also help create good airflow. A window in the door, and one at the opposite end should be enough to supply fresh air and control temperature in a small greenhouse. Install screens over the vents and windows to keep out any flying pests.

Using Your Greenhouse

Greenhouses constantly evolve in style and design, as do the tools and accessories to use within them. Manufacturers are constantly bringing to market more tools and accessories that will make work in greenhouses easier and quicker.

Many greenhouse enthusiasts are already using the ones we have just described. Part of the fun of greenhouse gardening is checking for newer and more efficient tools and methods!

Now that you're all set to go – greenhouse erected, staging in place, venting in place, and water readily available, it's time to make your plant decisions.

In spring and summer, food crops will likely dominate your greenhouse space.

Let's assume that you're planning to use your greenhouse to grow lots of delicious organic vegetables for your table. There are three basic methods for growing vegetables within the greenhouse. All work well, but each is distinct.

In a larger greenhouse, **raised beds around the inner perimeter** filled with enriched soil and well-rotted compost holds plants directly. This method saves work and money initially, but after a few years the soil will need to be removed and replaced. Watering is simple, with either an automated drip system or a drip hose.

Growing your plants in pots is also very simple and straightforward. Choose the right sized container for the adult plant, and place your pots around the border of the greenhouse where they'll get the most light. Watering is more hands-on with pots, and must be done daily in summer, unless you have a drip watering system in place.

Growing bags are now becoming a third and very popular alternative. These are simply bags of strong plastic filled with a good soil mix. Place the bags on a firm support, cut holes for your plants, and make sure you have drainage!

One to 4 seedlings can be planted in each bag. Staking or supporting the plants will be necessary as they grow. At season's end, remove the plants and add them to your compost. Empty the grow bags into your compost as well, or add the soil to your garden beds.

In spring, the greenhouse is a perfect place to propagate seedlings, pot up plants, and harden off more tender varieties. Early lettuce, Chinese greens, radishes and parsley can grace your tables, grown in your own space.

Later, cucumbers, melons, tomatoes and peppers will thrive in the warmth of summer within the greenhouse. In later summer, you can re-seed crops that winter well – chard, spinach, and other half-hardy vegetables.

If you grow carrots, beets, turnips and other root crops, plant them in deep boxes or in a perimeter raised bed at least 2 feet deep. Large individual tub-type containers suit tomatoes, cucumbers and pole beans, while lettuce, parsley, spinach or other low leafy vegetables can be planted in the tub around the taller vegetables.

"Let food by thy medicine and medicine be thy food"
Hippocrates

Miscellaneous Tips

- Use room temperature water to water your greenhouse plants. Let tap water stand for a day to get rid of chlorine and to warm up. A large tub, garbage can or 40-gallon drum is the perfect solution.

- Install a rain barrel to collect rainwater. It's a good investment, and very useful as a source of extra water.

- To make more room in your greenhouse, use the lower benches for starting seeds and transplants and the upper benches for growing flowers and specimen plants.

- Set aside one shelf or stage area for preparation, mixing soil and re-potting. This makes for a tidier greenhouse. Locate pots, trays and tools, ready to use, on a shelf below.

Greenhouses are plant shelters, a place for cultivating, growing and enjoying plants all year long, but also a refuge from outside stresses, and a healthy vocation for amateur and expert horticulturists.

Your greenhouse will be a welcome stress-buster from the hurried busyness of everyday life.

And once you've tasted fresh, juicy tomatoes or bright green lettuce, chard and kale "harvested" in your greenhouse weeks after the garden has been put to bed, you'll shun the bland and often wilted supermarket varieties that pale in comparison with your greenhouse babies.

Resources

For greenhouse tips covering topics such as: humidity, growing berries, opening a greenhouse business, fall greenhouse tips, and hanging baskets in the greenhouse, visit: **http://www.greenhouses.com/**.

This site sells many brands of pre-fabricated greenhouses as well as having a wealth of information.

Building your own greenhouse? This site has two basic plans: **http://www.floridagardener.com/greenhouse/greenhouseillustration1.htm**

Another site with greenhouse building plans and lot more information is:

http://www.123-greenhouse-gardening.com/free-greenhouse-plans.html

Ten plans, from very simple to elaborate for building a greenhouse can be found here:

http://www.renovation-headquarters.com/plans-greenhouse.htm

Books:

The Greenhouse Gardener's Companion Revised: Growing food or flowers in your greenhouse or sunspace. Shane Smith (Author). This is a comprehensive guide to greenhouse growing – one of the best available.

Building & Using Cold Frames: Garden Way Publishing Bulletin A-39 [Paperback], Charles Siegchrist (Author) All you'll need to know to build your own cold frames.

Websites:

The Internet has many sites that have good information about greenhouse building and growing, and sources of quality products. Here are just a few.

www.motherearthnews.com

http://www.johnnyseeds.com/t-protected-culture-greenhouse-growing-basics.aspx

www.greenhousegarden.com

http://www.planetnatural.com/greenhouse-kits/

http://www.greenhousecatalog.com/greenhouse-selection

Check with online marketplaces like EBay and Amazon for both products and books.

Amazon offers a vast array of products to protect your plants, from single cloches to large greenhouses. Visit your country's Amazon site to check what they have on offer.

About the Author

Nicolette Goff was born in British Columbia's Rocky Mountains. Growing up on a small farm (one of 9 children) in the '50's, organic gardening became important part of her life, and continues to be one of her passions today. Gardening naturally led to an interest in cooking healthy meals and exploring different cuisines.

Her experiences and adventures as an elementary school teacher and librarian for 12 years expanded her passion for learning, traveling and writing.

Currently living on beautiful Vancouver Island, Nicolette enjoys travel, hiking, painting, writing, reading, cooking and having fun with her 2 daughters and 3 grandchildren.

More by Nicolette Goff:

All books are available on Amazon, as e-book editions.

The Healthy Quinoa Cookbook

Easy Quinoa Recipes – a Bakers' Dozen

Growing Culinary Herbs

Herbs for Health and Healing

How to Preserve and Enjoy Your Garden Herbs

Printed in Great Britain
by Amazon

67750646R00037